Anger Management
Journal with Prompts

Dedication

This Anger Management Workbook Journal is dedicated to all the people out there who want to improve their anger management skills and document their findings in the process.

You are my inspiration for producing books and I'm honored to be a part of keeping all of your Anger Management notes and records organized.

This journal notebook will help you record your details about your anger.

Thoughtfully put together with these sections to record in detail: Triggers, Anger Inventory, Anger Meter, and My Daily Commitment Contract.

How to Use this Book

The purpose of this book is to keep all of your Anger Management notes all in one place. It will help keep you organized.

This Anger Management Journal will allow you to accurately document every detail about your anger. It's a great way to chart your course through working on your anger issues.

Here are examples of the prompts for you to fill in and write about your experience in this book:

1. Triggers - Fill in the checklist of what triggers your anger.

2. Anger Inventory - Write the Incident, Date Where, Comments

3. Anger Meter - Fill in on the thermometer, how high your anger was.

4. My Daily Commitment Contract - Sign the contract stating you will behave in a calmy and non-aggressive manner. Also space for a witness to sign.

Getting to know your anger a bit more

What does anger look like? Draw it in the space below:

Getting to know your anger a bit more

What does anger smell like?

_____
_____
_____

What does sound smell like?

_____
_____
_____

What does feel like?

_____
_____
_____

Getting to know your anger a bit more

If anger was a character from a book or TV show, what would it be?

_____
_____
_____
_____

If your anger had a motto, what would it be?

_____
_____
_____
_____

What's the #1 thing you want to achieve through anger management?

_____
_____
_____
_____

What triggers your anger?

- ❏ Bad news
- ❏ Being told "No"
- ❏ Waiting awhile
- ❏ Hunger
- ❏ Cheating
- ❏ A misunderstanding
- ❏ Being ignored
- ❏ Too much to do
- ❏ Being disrespected
- ❏ Loud noises
- ❏ Being told what to do
- ❏ Exhaustion
- ❏ Being left out
- ❏ Rumors or gossip
- ❏ Unfair treatment
- ❏ Hurt or pain
- ❏ Being touched
- ❏ Being bumped into
- ❏ Losing a game
- ❏ An accident
- ❏ Being late

What triggers your anger?

- ❏ Being scared
- ❏ Being criticized
- ❏ Things are not fair
- ❏ An interruption
- ❏ Things not going as planned
- ❏ Certain people
- ❏ Not understanding what to do
- ❏ Trauma
- ❏ Bad memories
- ❏ Others (please specify):

Anger Inventory

Think of a time when you felt angry. Then, choose the responses that best describe these incidents and how you dealt with it. Feel free to add comments and reflections.

When?	Where?
Date: _____	❏ At home
❏ Morning	❏ At work
❏ Afternoon	❏ In the community
❏ Evening	Comments:
❏ Night	
Comments:	

_____

_____

_____

_____

_____

_____

_____

_____

_____

_____

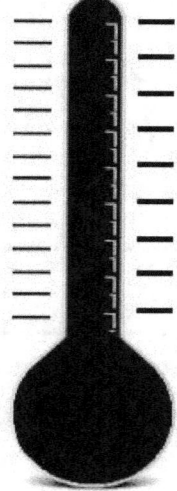

Anger Meter
Mark how angry you were

What happened?
- ❏ You did something wrong
- ❏ Somebody said something
- ❏ Somebody did something
- ❏ You were bossed around by somebody
- ❏ Someone treated you unfairly
- ❏ You did not get what you wanted
- ❏ Something else:

What did you do?
- ❏ Yelled
- ❏ Acted in a violent way
- ❏ Cursed
- ❏ Threw something
- ❏ Talked to somebody about it
- ❏ Showed assertiveness
- ❏ Walked away
- ❏ Did payback time to the person later on
- ❏ Something else:

Anger Inventory

Think of a time when you felt angry. Then, choose the responses that best describe these incidents and how you dealt with it. Feel free to add comments and reflections.

When?
Date: _____
- ❏ Morning
- ❏ Afternoon
- ❏ Evening
- ❏ Night

Comments:
_____
_____
_____
_____
_____

Where?
- ❏ At home
- ❏ At work
- ❏ In the community

Comments:
_____
_____
_____
_____
_____
_____

Anger Meter
Mark how angry you were

What happened?
- ☐ You did something wrong
- ☐ Somebody said something
- ☐ Somebody did something
- ☐ You were bossed around by somebody
- ☐ Someone treated you unfairly
- ☐ You did not get what you wanted
- ☐ Something else:

What did you do?
- ☐ Yelled
- ☐ Acted in a violent way
- ☐ Cursed
- ☐ Threw something
- ☐ Talked to somebody about it
- ☐ Showed assertiveness
- ☐ Walked away
- ☐ Did payback time to the person later on
- ☐ Something else:

Anger Inventory

Think of a time when you felt angry. Then, choose the responses that best describe these incidents and how you dealt with it. Feel free to add comments and reflections.

When?
Date: _____
- ❏ Morning
- ❏ Afternoon
- ❏ Evening
- ❏ Night

Comments:
_____
_____
_____
_____
_____

Where?
- ❏ At home
- ❏ At work
- ❏ In the community

Comments:
_____
_____
_____
_____
_____
_____
_____

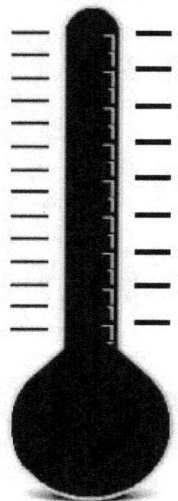

Anger Meter
Mark how angry you were

What happened?
- ❏ You did something wrong
- ❏ Somebody said something
- ❏ Somebody did something
- ❏ You were bossed around by somebody
- ❏ Someone treated you unfairly
- ❏ You did not get what you wanted
- ❏ Something else:

_____

_____

_____

_____

What did you do?
- ❏ Yelled
- ❏ Acted in a violent way
- ❏ Cursed
- ❏ Threw something
- ❏ Talked to somebody about it
- ❏ Showed assertiveness
- ❏ Walked away
- ❏ Did payback time to the person later on
- ❏ Something else:

_____

_____

_____

_____

_____

Anger Inventory

Think of a time when you felt angry. Then, choose the responses that best describe these incidents and how you dealt with it. Feel free to add comments and reflections.

When?
Date: _____
- ❏ Morning
- ❏ Afternoon
- ❏ Evening
- ❏ Night

Comments:
_____
_____
_____
_____
_____

Where?
- ❏ At home
- ❏ At work
- ❏ In the community

Comments:
_____
_____
_____
_____
_____
_____
_____

Anger Meter
Mark how angry you were

What happened?
- ☐ You did something wrong
- ☐ Somebody said something
- ☐ Somebody did something
- ☐ You were bossed around by somebody
- ☐ Someone treated you unfairly
- ☐ You did not get what you wanted
- ☐ Something else:

_____

_____

_____

_____

What did you do?
- ☐ Yelled
- ☐ Acted in a violent way
- ☐ Cursed
- ☐ Threw something
- ☐ Talked to somebody about it
- ☐ Showed assertiveness
- ☐ Walked away
- ☐ Did payback time to the person later on
- ☐ Something else:

_____

_____

_____

_____

_____

Anger Inventory

Think of a time when you felt angry. Then, choose the responses that best describe these incidents and how you dealt with it. Feel free to add comments and reflections.

When?
Date: _____
- ❏ Morning
- ❏ Afternoon
- ❏ Evening
- ❏ Night

Comments:
_____
_____
_____
_____
_____

Where?
- ❏ At home
- ❏ At work
- ❏ In the community

Comments:
_____
_____
_____
_____
_____
_____
_____

Anger Meter
Mark how angry you were

What happened?
- ❏ You did something wrong
- ❏ Somebody said something
- ❏ Somebody did something
- ❏ You were bossed around by somebody
- ❏ Someone treated you unfairly
- ❏ You did not get what you wanted
- ❏ Something else:

What did you do?
- ❏ Yelled
- ❏ Acted in a violent way
- ❏ Cursed
- ❏ Threw something
- ❏ Talked to somebody about it
- ❏ Showed assertiveness
- ❏ Walked away
- ❏ Did payback time to the person later on
- ❏ Something else:

Anger Inventory

Think of a time when you felt angry. Then, choose the responses that best describe these incidents and how you dealt with it. Feel free to add comments and reflections.

When?
Date: _____
- ❏ Morning
- ❏ Afternoon
- ❏ Evening
- ❏ Night

Comments:
_____
_____
_____
_____
_____

Where?
- ❏ At home
- ❏ At work
- ❏ In the community

Comments:
_____
_____
_____
_____
_____
_____
_____

Anger Meter
Mark how angry you were

What happened?
- ❏ You did something wrong
- ❏ Somebody said something
- ❏ Somebody did something
- ❏ You were bossed around by somebody
- ❏ Someone treated you unfairly
- ❏ You did not get what you wanted
- ❏ Something else:

What did you do?
- ❏ Yelled
- ❏ Acted in a violent way
- ❏ Cursed
- ❏ Threw something
- ❏ Talked to somebody about it
- ❏ Showed assertiveness
- ❏ Walked away
- ❏ Did payback time to the person later on
- ❏ Something else:

Anger Inventory

Think of a time when you felt angry. Then, choose the responses that best describe these incidents and how you dealt with it. Feel free to add comments and reflections.

When?
Date: _____
- ❏ Morning
- ❏ Afternoon
- ❏ Evening
- ❏ Night

Comments:
_____
_____
_____
_____
_____
_____

Where?
- ❏ At home
- ❏ At work
- ❏ In the community

Comments:
_____
_____
_____
_____
_____
_____
_____

Anger Meter
Mark how angry you were

What happened?
- ❏ You did something wrong
- ❏ Somebody said something
- ❏ Somebody did something
- ❏ You were bossed around by somebody
- ❏ Someone treated you unfairly
- ❏ You did not get what you wanted
- ❏ Something else:

What did you do?
- ❏ Yelled
- ❏ Acted in a violent way
- ❏ Cursed
- ❏ Threw something
- ❏ Talked to somebody about it
- ❏ Showed assertiveness
- ❏ Walked away
- ❏ Did payback time to the person later on
- ❏ Something else:

Anger Inventory

Think of a time when you felt angry. Then, choose the responses that best describe these incidents and how you dealt with it. Feel free to add comments and reflections.

When?	Where?
Date: _____	❏ At home
❏ Morning	❏ At work
❏ Afternoon	❏ In the community
❏ Evening	Comments:
❏ Night	_____
Comments:	_____
_____	_____
_____	_____
_____	_____
_____	_____
_____	_____
_____	_____

Anger Meter
Mark how angry you were

What happened?
- ❑ You did something wrong
- ❑ Somebody said something
- ❑ Somebody did something
- ❑ You were bossed around by somebody
- ❑ Someone treated you unfairly
- ❑ You did not get what you wanted
- ❑ Something else:

What did you do?
- ❑ Yelled
- ❑ Acted in a violent way
- ❑ Cursed
- ❑ Threw something
- ❑ Talked to somebody about it
- ❑ Showed assertiveness
- ❑ Walked away
- ❑ Did payback time to the person later on
- ❑ Something else:

Anger Inventory

Think of a time when you felt angry. Then, choose the responses that best describe these incidents and how you dealt with it. Feel free to add comments and reflections.

When?	Where?
Date: _____	❏ At home
❏ Morning	❏ At work
❏ Afternoon	❏ In the community
❏ Evening	Comments:
❏ Night	
Comments:	

Anger Meter
Mark how angry you were

What happened?
- ❏ You did something wrong
- ❏ Somebody said something
- ❏ Somebody did something
- ❏ You were bossed around by somebody
- ❏ Someone treated you unfairly
- ❏ You did not get what you wanted
- ❏ Something else:

What did you do?
- ❏ Yelled
- ❏ Acted in a violent way
- ❏ Cursed
- ❏ Threw something
- ❏ Talked to somebody about it
- ❏ Showed assertiveness
- ❏ Walked away
- ❏ Did payback time to the person later on
- ❏ Something else:

Anger Inventory

Think of a time when you felt angry. Then, choose the responses that best describe these incidents and how you dealt with it. Feel free to add comments and reflections.

When?
Date: _____
- ❏ Morning
- ❏ Afternoon
- ❏ Evening
- ❏ Night

Comments:

_____

_____

_____

_____

_____

Where?
- ❏ At home
- ❏ At work
- ❏ In the community

Comments:

_____

_____

_____

_____

_____

_____

Anger Meter
Mark how angry you were

What happened?
- ❏ You did something wrong
- ❏ Somebody said something
- ❏ Somebody did something
- ❏ You were bossed around by somebody
- ❏ Someone treated you unfairly
- ❏ You did not get what you wanted
- ❏ Something else:

What did you do?
- ❏ Yelled
- ❏ Acted in a violent way
- ❏ Cursed
- ❏ Threw something
- ❏ Talked to somebody about it
- ❏ Showed assertiveness
- ❏ Walked away
- ❏ Did payback time to the person later on
- ❏ Something else:

Anger Inventory

Think of a time when you felt angry. Then, choose the responses that best describe these incidents and how you dealt with it. Feel free to add comments and reflections.

When?
Date: _____
- ❏ Morning
- ❏ Afternoon
- ❏ Evening
- ❏ Night

Comments:
_____
_____
_____
_____
_____

Where?
- ❏ At home
- ❏ At work
- ❏ In the community

Comments:
_____
_____
_____
_____
_____
_____
_____

Anger Meter
Mark how angry you were

What happened?
- ❏ You did something wrong
- ❏ Somebody said something
- ❏ Somebody did something
- ❏ You were bossed around by somebody
- ❏ Someone treated you unfairly
- ❏ You did not get what you wanted
- ❏ Something else:

What did you do?
- ❏ Yelled
- ❏ Acted in a violent way
- ❏ Cursed
- ❏ Threw something
- ❏ Talked to somebody about it
- ❏ Showed assertiveness
- ❏ Walked away
- ❏ Did payback time to the person later on
- ❏ Something else:

Anger Inventory

Think of a time when you felt angry. Then, choose the responses that best describe these incidents and how you dealt with it. Feel free to add comments and reflections.

When?
Date: _____
- ❏ Morning
- ❏ Afternoon
- ❏ Evening
- ❏ Night

Comments:
_____
_____
_____
_____
_____

Where?
- ❏ At home
- ❏ At work
- ❏ In the community

Comments:
_____
_____
_____
_____
_____
_____
_____

Anger Meter
Mark how angry you were

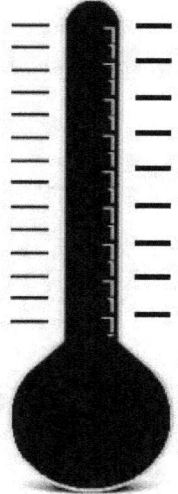

What happened?
- ❏ You did something wrong
- ❏ Somebody said something
- ❏ Somebody did something
- ❏ You were bossed around by somebody
- ❏ Someone treated you unfairly
- ❏ You did not get what you wanted
- ❏ Something else:

What did you do?
- ❏ Yelled
- ❏ Acted in a violent way
- ❏ Cursed
- ❏ Threw something
- ❏ Talked to somebody about it
- ❏ Showed assertiveness
- ❏ Walked away
- ❏ Did payback time to the person later on
- ❏ Something else:

Anger Inventory

Think of a time when you felt angry. Then, choose the responses that best describe these incidents and how you dealt with it. Feel free to add comments and reflections.

When?
Date: _____
- ❏ Morning
- ❏ Afternoon
- ❏ Evening
- ❏ Night

Comments:
_____
_____
_____
_____
_____

Where?
- ❏ At home
- ❏ At work
- ❏ In the community

Comments:
_____
_____
_____
_____
_____
_____

Anger Meter
Mark how angry you were

What happened?
- ❏ You did something wrong
- ❏ Somebody said something
- ❏ Somebody did something
- ❏ You were bossed around by somebody
- ❏ Someone treated you unfairly
- ❏ You did not get what you wanted
- ❏ Something else:

_____

_____

_____

_____

What did you do?
- ❏ Yelled
- ❏ Acted in a violent way
- ❏ Cursed
- ❏ Threw something
- ❏ Talked to somebody about it
- ❏ Showed assertiveness
- ❏ Walked away
- ❏ Did payback time to the person later on
- ❏ Something else:

_____

_____

_____

_____

_____

Anger Inventory

Think of a time when you felt angry. Then, choose the responses that best describe these incidents and how you dealt with it. Feel free to add comments and reflections.

When?
Date: _____
- ❏ Morning
- ❏ Afternoon
- ❏ Evening
- ❏ Night

Comments:
_____
_____
_____
_____
_____

Where?
- ❏ At home
- ❏ At work
- ❏ In the community

Comments:
_____
_____
_____
_____
_____
_____

Anger Meter
Mark how angry you were

What happened?
- ❏ You did something wrong
- ❏ Somebody said something
- ❏ Somebody did something
- ❏ You were bossed around by somebody
- ❏ Someone treated you unfairly
- ❏ You did not get what you wanted
- ❏ Something else:

What did you do?
- ❏ Yelled
- ❏ Acted in a violent way
- ❏ Cursed
- ❏ Threw something
- ❏ Talked to somebody about it
- ❏ Showed assertiveness
- ❏ Walked away
- ❏ Did payback time to the person later on
- ❏ Something else:

Anger Inventory

Think of a time when you felt angry. Then, choose the responses that best describe these incidents and how you dealt with it. Feel free to add comments and reflections.

When?
Date: _____
- ❏ Morning
- ❏ Afternoon
- ❏ Evening
- ❏ Night

Comments:
_____
_____
_____
_____
_____

Where?
- ❏ At home
- ❏ At work
- ❏ In the community

Comments:
_____
_____
_____
_____
_____
_____
_____

Anger Meter
Mark how angry you were

What happened?
- ❏ You did something wrong
- ❏ Somebody said something
- ❏ Somebody did something
- ❏ You were bossed around by somebody
- ❏ Someone treated you unfairly
- ❏ You did not get what you wanted
- ❏ Something else:

What did you do?
- ❏ Yelled
- ❏ Acted in a violent way
- ❏ Cursed
- ❏ Threw something
- ❏ Talked to somebody about it
- ❏ Showed assertiveness
- ❏ Walked away
- ❏ Did payback time to the person later on
- ❏ Something else:

Anger Inventory

Think of a time when you felt angry. Then, choose the responses that best describe these incidents and how you dealt with it. Feel free to add comments and reflections.

When?
Date: _____
- ❏ Morning
- ❏ Afternoon
- ❏ Evening
- ❏ Night

Comments:
_____
_____
_____
_____

Where?
- ❏ At home
- ❏ At work
- ❏ In the community

Comments:
_____
_____
_____
_____
_____

Anger Meter
Mark how angry you were

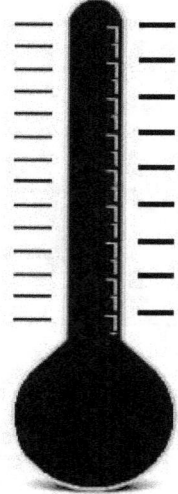

What happened?
- ❏ You did something wrong
- ❏ Somebody said something
- ❏ Somebody did something
- ❏ You were bossed around by somebody
- ❏ Someone treated you unfairly
- ❏ You did not get what you wanted
- ❏ Something else:

What did you do?
- ❏ Yelled
- ❏ Acted in a violent way
- ❏ Cursed
- ❏ Threw something
- ❏ Talked to somebody about it
- ❏ Showed assertiveness
- ❏ Walked away
- ❏ Did payback time to the person later on
- ❏ Something else:

Anger Inventory

Think of a time when you felt angry. Then, choose the responses that best describe these incidents and how you dealt with it. Feel free to add comments and reflections.

When?
Date: _____
- ❏ Morning
- ❏ Afternoon
- ❏ Evening
- ❏ Night

Comments:
_____
_____
_____
_____
_____

Where?
- ❏ At home
- ❏ At work
- ❏ In the community

Comments:
_____
_____
_____
_____
_____
_____
_____

Anger Meter
Mark how angry you were

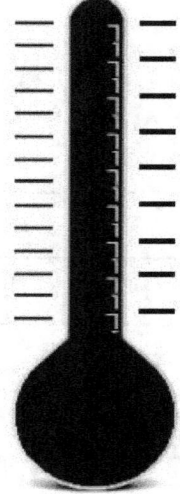

What happened?
- ❏ You did something wrong
- ❏ Somebody said something
- ❏ Somebody did something
- ❏ You were bossed around by somebody
- ❏ Someone treated you unfairly
- ❏ You did not get what you wanted
- ❏ Something else:

What did you do?
- ❏ Yelled
- ❏ Acted in a violent way
- ❏ Cursed
- ❏ Threw something
- ❏ Talked to somebody about it
- ❏ Showed assertiveness
- ❏ Walked away
- ❏ Did payback time to the person later on
- ❏ Something else:

Anger Inventory

Think of a time when you felt angry. Then, choose the responses that best describe these incidents and how you dealt with it. Feel free to add comments and reflections.

When?	Where?
Date: _____	❏ At home
❏ Morning	❏ At work
❏ Afternoon	❏ In the community
❏ Evening	Comments:
❏ Night	
Comments:	

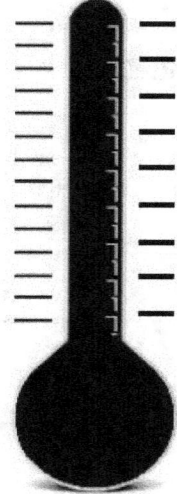

Anger Meter
Mark how angry you were

What happened?
- ❏ You did something wrong
- ❏ Somebody said something
- ❏ Somebody did something
- ❏ You were bossed around by somebody
- ❏ Someone treated you unfairly
- ❏ You did not get what you wanted
- ❏ Something else:

What did you do?
- ❏ Yelled
- ❏ Acted in a violent way
- ❏ Cursed
- ❏ Threw something
- ❏ Talked to somebody about it
- ❏ Showed assertiveness
- ❏ Walked away
- ❏ Did payback time to the person later on
- ❏ Something else:

Anger Inventory

Think of a time when you felt angry. Then, choose the responses that best describe these incidents and how you dealt with it. Feel free to add comments and reflections.

When?
Date: _____
- ❏ Morning
- ❏ Afternoon
- ❏ Evening
- ❏ Night

Comments:
_____
_____
_____
_____
_____

Where?
- ❏ At home
- ❏ At work
- ❏ In the community

Comments:
_____
_____
_____
_____
_____
_____

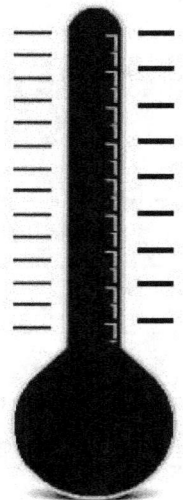

Anger Meter
Mark how angry you were

What happened?
- ❏ You did something wrong
- ❏ Somebody said something
- ❏ Somebody did something
- ❏ You were bossed around by somebody
- ❏ Someone treated you unfairly
- ❏ You did not get what you wanted
- ❏ Something else:

What did you do?
- ❏ Yelled
- ❏ Acted in a violent way
- ❏ Cursed
- ❏ Threw something
- ❏ Talked to somebody about it
- ❏ Showed assertiveness
- ❏ Walked away
- ❏ Did payback time to the person later on
- ❏ Something else:

Anger Inventory

Think of a time when you felt angry. Then, choose the responses that best describe these incidents and how you dealt with it. Feel free to add comments and reflections.

When?
Date: _____
- ❑ Morning
- ❑ Afternoon
- ❑ Evening
- ❑ Night

Comments:
_____
_____
_____
_____
_____
_____

Where?
- ❑ At home
- ❑ At work
- ❑ In the community

Comments:
_____
_____
_____
_____
_____
_____
_____

Anger Meter
Mark how angry you were

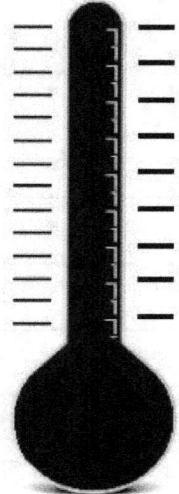

What happened?
- ❏ You did something wrong
- ❏ Somebody said something
- ❏ Somebody did something
- ❏ You were bossed around by somebody
- ❏ Someone treated you unfairly
- ❏ You did not get what you wanted
- ❏ Something else:

What did you do?
- ❏ Yelled
- ❏ Acted in a violent way
- ❏ Cursed
- ❏ Threw something
- ❏ Talked to somebody about it
- ❏ Showed assertiveness
- ❏ Walked away
- ❏ Did payback time to the person later on
- ❏ Something else:

Anger Inventory

Think of a time when you felt angry. Then, choose the responses that best describe these incidents and how you dealt with it. Feel free to add comments and reflections.

When?	Where?
Date: _____	❑ At home
❑ Morning	❑ At work
❑ Afternoon	❑ In the community
❑ Evening	Comments:
❑ Night	
Comments:	

Anger Meter
Mark how angry you were

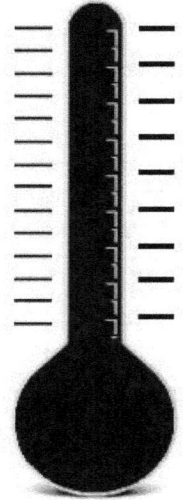

What happened?
- ☐ You did something wrong
- ☐ Somebody said something
- ☐ Somebody did something
- ☐ You were bossed around by somebody
- ☐ Someone treated you unfairly
- ☐ You did not get what you wanted
- ☐ Something else:

_____

_____

_____

_____

What did you do?
- ☐ Yelled
- ☐ Acted in a violent way
- ☐ Cursed
- ☐ Threw something
- ☐ Talked to somebody about it
- ☐ Showed assertiveness
- ☐ Walked away
- ☐ Did payback time to the person later on
- ☐ Something else:

_____

_____

_____

_____

Anger Inventory

Think of a time when you felt angry. Then, choose the responses that best describe these incidents and how you dealt with it. Feel free to add comments and reflections.

When?	Where?
Date: _____	❏ At home
❏ Morning	❏ At work
❏ Afternoon	❏ In the community
❏ Evening	Comments:
❏ Night	
Comments:	

Anger Meter
Mark how angry you were

What happened?
- ❏ You did something wrong
- ❏ Somebody said something
- ❏ Somebody did something
- ❏ You were bossed around by somebody
- ❏ Someone treated you unfairly
- ❏ You did not get what you wanted
- ❏ Something else:

What did you do?
- ❏ Yelled
- ❏ Acted in a violent way
- ❏ Cursed
- ❏ Threw something
- ❏ Talked to somebody about it
- ❏ Showed assertiveness
- ❏ Walked away
- ❏ Did payback time to the person later on
- ❏ Something else:

My commitment to acting calm

Tell you friends about your call to action. Give family & friends a non-verbal signal they can use to let you know if you're looking or sounding angry.

Write and explain the gesture below:

My daily commitment

Sign a contract and have a close family or friend sign as witness to the contract. At the end of each day, write down comments, reflections, and how you can improve as days go by.

Daily Contract to Act Calm

I, _____, on _____ (date), promise to behave in a calm and non-aggressive manner. I will act calmly despite the stress or provocations that may occur.

_____
Your Signature

_____
Witness Signature

Comments, Reflections, Things I Can Improve On

My daily commitment

Sign a contract and have a close family or friend sign as witness to the contract. At the end of each day, write down comments, reflections, and how you can improve as days go by.

Daily Contract to Act Calm

I, _____, on _____ (date), promise to behave in a calm and non-aggressive manner. I will act calmly despite the stress or provocations that may occur.

_____
Your Signature

_____
Witness Signature

Comments, Reflections, Things I Can Improve On

My daily commitment

Sign a contract and have a close family or friend sign as witness to the contract. At the end of each day, write down comments, reflections, and how you can improve as days go by.

Daily Contract to Act Calm

I, _____, on _____ (date), promise to behave in a calm and non-aggressive manner. I will act calmly despite the stress or provocations that may occur.

Your Signature

Witness Signature

Comments, Reflections, Things I Can Improve On

My daily commitment

Sign a contract and have a close family or friend sign as witness to the contract. At the end of each day, write down comments, reflections, and how you can improve as days go by.

Daily Contract to Act Calm

I, _____, on _____ (date), promise to behave in a calm and non-aggressive manner. I will act calmly despite the stress or provocations that may occur.

_____
Your Signature

_____
Witness Signature

Comments, Reflections, Things I Can Improve On

My daily commitment

Sign a contract and have a close family or friend sign as witness to the contract. At the end of each day, write down comments, reflections, and how you can improve as days go by.

Daily Contract to Act Calm

I, _____, on _____ (date), promise to behave in a calm and non-aggressive manner. I will act calmly despite the stress or provocations that may occur.

_____
Your Signature

_____
Witness Signature

Comments, Reflections, Things I Can Improve On

My daily commitment

Sign a contract and have a close family or friend sign as witness to the contract. At the end of each day, write down comments, reflections, and how you can improve as days go by.

Daily Contract to Act Calm

I, _____, on _____ (date), promise to behave in a calm and non-aggressive manner. I will act calmly despite the stress or provocations that may occur.

_____
Your Signature

_____
Witness Signature

Comments, Reflections, Things I Can Improve On

My daily commitment

Sign a contract and have a close family or friend sign as witness to the contract. At the end of each day, write down comments, reflections, and how you can improve as days go by.

Daily Contract to Act Calm

I, _____, on _____ (date), promise to behave in a calm and non-aggressive manner. I will act calmly despite the stress or provocations that may occur.

_____
Your Signature

_____
Witness Signature

Comments, Reflections, Things I Can Improve On

My daily commitment

Sign a contract and have a close family or friend sign as witness to the contract. At the end of each day, write down comments, reflections, and how you can improve as days go by.

Daily Contract to Act Calm

I, _____, on _____ (date), promise to behave in a calm and non-aggressive manner. I will act calmly despite the stress or provocations that may occur.

_____
Your Signature

_____
Witness Signature

Comments, Reflections, Things I Can Improve On

My daily commitment

Sign a contract and have a close family or friend sign as witness to the contract. At the end of each day, write down comments, reflections, and how you can improve as days go by.

Daily Contract to Act Calm

I, _____, on _____ (date), promise to behave in a calm and non-aggressive manner. I will act calmly despite the stress or provocations that may occur.

_____
Your Signature

_____
Witness Signature

Comments, Reflections, Things I Can Improve On

My daily commitment

Sign a contract and have a close family or friend sign as witness to the contract. At the end of each day, write down comments, reflections, and how you can improve as days go by.

Daily Contract to Act Calm

I, _____, on _____ (date), promise to behave in a calm and non-aggressive manner. I will act calmly despite the stress or provocations that may occur.

_____
Your Signature

_____
Witness Signature

Comments, Reflections, Things I Can Improve On

My daily commitment

Sign a contract and have a close family or friend sign as witness to the contract. At the end of each day, write down comments, reflections, and how you can improve as days go by.

Daily Contract to Act Calm

I, _____, on _____ (date), promise to behave in a calm and non-aggressive manner. I will act calmly despite the stress or provocations that may occur.

_____
Your Signature

_____
Witness Signature

Comments, Reflections, Things I Can Improve On

My daily commitment

Sign a contract and have a close family or friend sign as witness to the contract. At the end of each day, write down comments, reflections, and how you can improve as days go by.

Daily Contract to Act Calm

I, _____, on _____ (date), promise to behave in a calm and non-aggressive manner. I will act calmly despite the stress or provocations that may occur.

_____
Your Signature

_____
Witness Signature

Comments, Reflections, Things I Can Improve On

My daily commitment

Sign a contract and have a close family or friend sign as witness to the contract. At the end of each day, write down comments, reflections, and how you can improve as days go by.

Daily Contract to Act Calm

I, _____, on _____ (date), promise to behave in a calm and non-aggressive manner. I will act calmly despite the stress or provocations that may occur.

_____
Your Signature

_____
Witness Signature

Comments, Reflections, Things I Can Improve On

My daily commitment

Sign a contract and have a close family or friend sign as witness to the contract. At the end of each day, write down comments, reflections, and how you can improve as days go by.

Daily Contract to Act Calm

I, _____, on _____ (date), promise to behave in a calm and non-aggressive manner. I will act calmly despite the stress or provocations that may occur.

_____
Your Signature

_____
Witness Signature

Comments, Reflections, Things I Can Improve On

My daily commitment

Sign a contract and have a close family or friend sign as witness to the contract. At the end of each day, write down comments, reflections, and how you can improve as days go by.

Daily Contract to Act Calm

I, _____, on _____ (date), promise to behave in a calm and non-aggressive manner. I will act calmly despite the stress or provocations that may occur.

_____
Your Signature

_____
Witness Signature

Comments, Reflections, Things I Can Improve On

My daily commitment

Sign a contract and have a close family or friend sign as witness to the contract. At the end of each day, write down comments, reflections, and how you can improve as days go by.

Daily Contract to Act Calm

I, _____, on _____ (date), promise to behave in a calm and non-aggressive manner. I will act calmly despite the stress or provocations that may occur.

Your Signature

Witness Signature

Comments, Reflections, Things I Can Improve On

My daily commitment

Sign a contract and have a close family or friend sign as witness to the contract. At the end of each day, write down comments, reflections, and how you can improve as days go by.

Daily Contract to Act Calm

I, _____, on _____ (date), promise to behave in a calm and non-aggressive manner. I will act calmly despite the stress or provocations that may occur.

_____
Your Signature

_____
Witness Signature

Comments, Reflections, Things I Can Improve On

My daily commitment

Sign a contract and have a close family or friend sign as witness to the contract. At the end of each day, write down comments, reflections, and how you can improve as days go by.

Daily Contract to Act Calm

I, _____, on _____ (date), promise to behave in a calm and non-aggressive manner. I will act calmly despite the stress or provocations that may occur.

_____
Your Signature

_____
Witness Signature

Comments, Reflections, Things I Can Improve On

My daily commitment

Sign a contract and have a close family or friend sign as witness to the contract. At the end of each day, write down comments, reflections, and how you can improve as days go by.

Daily Contract to Act Calm

I, _____, on _____ (date), promise to behave in a calm and non-aggressive manner. I will act calmly despite the stress or provocations that may occur.

_____
Your Signature

_____
Witness Signature

Comments, Reflections, Things I Can Improve On

My daily commitment

Sign a contract and have a close family or friend sign as witness to the contract. At the end of each day, write down comments, reflections, and how you can improve as days go by.

Daily Contract to Act Calm

I, _____, on _____ (date), promise to behave in a calm and non-aggressive manner. I will act calmly despite the stress or provocations that may occur.

_____
Your Signature

_____
Witness Signature

Comments, Reflections, Things I Can Improve On

My daily commitment

Sign a contract and have a close family or friend sign as witness to the contract. At the end of each day, write down comments, reflections, and how you can improve as days go by.

Daily Contract to Act Calm

I, _____, on _____ (date), promise to behave in a calm and non-aggressive manner. I will act calmly despite the stress or provocations that may occur.

_____
Your Signature

_____
Witness Signature

Comments, Reflections, Things I Can Improve On

My daily commitment

Sign a contract and have a close family or friend sign as witness to the contract. At the end of each day, write down comments, reflections, and how you can improve as days go by.

Daily Contract to Act Calm

I, _____, on _____ (date), promise to behave in a calm and non-aggressive manner. I will act calmly despite the stress or provocations that may occur.

_____
Your Signature

_____
Witness Signature

Comments, Reflections, Things I Can Improve On

My daily commitment

Sign a contract and have a close family or friend sign as witness to the contract. At the end of each day, write down comments, reflections, and how you can improve as days go by.

Daily Contract to Act Calm

I, _____, on _____ (date), promise to behave in a calm and non-aggressive manner. I will act calmly despite the stress or provocations that may occur.

_____
Your Signature

_____
Witness Signature

Comments, Reflections, Things I Can Improve On

My daily commitment

Sign a contract and have a close family or friend sign as witness to the contract. At the end of each day, write down comments, reflections, and how you can improve as days go by.

Daily Contract to Act Calm

I, _____, on _____ (date), promise to behave in a calm and non-aggressive manner. I will act calmly despite the stress or provocations that may occur.

_____
Your Signature

_____
Witness Signature

Comments, Reflections, Things I Can Improve On

www.ingramcontent.com/pod-product-compliance
Lightning Source LLC
Chambersburg PA
CBHW071405080526
44587CB00017B/3183